SHUSH! IT'S A SECRET,
THE LAKE HIDES HIS DUMMY

PART OF THE RAINBOW OF LIFE'S SECRETS SERIES

By

TORRY FOUNTINHEAD

AIRÉ LIBRÉ PUBLISHING & COMPUTING LTD.

For more information contact:
Airé Libré Publishing & Computing Ltd.
Suite 306, 185-911 Yates St.
Victoria BC V8V 4Y9 Canada
Tel: 1-250-592-3099.
Http://www.al.bc.ca info@al.bc.ca

AL

Published by:
Airé Libré Publishing & Computing Ltd.
http://www.al.bc.ca
Book Design © Torry Fountinhead
ISBN-10: 0-9781498-9-0
ISBN-13: 978-0-9781498-9-5

Shush! It's a Secret, The Lake Hides His Dummy
ISBN-10 0-9781498-9-0
ISBN-13 978-0-9781498-9-5

51799

9 780978 149895

Dedicated

To Lior

With Love...

What is it about babies
They love their soothers
And don't want to be without them
Even if they just hold them

Like old friends

Their soother brings them joy

Comfort of being satisfied

From a look-a-like

2

My boy, now a big man
Also loved his soother
That was called *Dummy*
They were inseparable

3

We had a few of them
So he won't be without
He was very unhappy
If his Dummy friend was not around

You had to see him
Smiling face and full of joy
Holding his Dummy with his teeth
And then popping it out with a loud noise

5

When he was tired, my boy

He not only sucked his Dummy

But he would hold it tightly

So his whole face would feel it

Like this, three years have past
And I was worried that he will never say Goodbye
You see, his teeth started to take the shape of his
Dummy, What could be done?

My boy was smart, and so I thought

Let's make up a story

Where he and Dummy can say Goodbye

Because there was a need to

So one day I called my son
And told him about the big man
That collects all the Dummies
And takes them away when their time comes

My boy cried: away where?

His face so unhappy

And I said the truth

That – I don't know

But I told my boy

That I thought of a good solution

To out smart the big man

And hide all his Dummies

Happiness now was showing

On my boy's beautiful face

Mischievous smile was forming

And his naughtiness was building up

He was all anticipation
You could feel his bubbling energy
Almost about to explode, he shouted
How? How? How?

I smiled at his eager face

Feeling my heart melting with love for him

He would never know

His mother's efforts for his happiness

Well, I made it even more interesting
I took him to one of the large lakes
In the beautiful area where we lived
I wanted it to be real and easy to understand

So, here we are walking right to the edge

Then, entered the shallow water

I asked my boy to look in and see

The underwater forest-like plants

There were small fish going about
It looked so peaceful yet active
And then I pointed out a small rock
All covered with algae, almost hidden from view

I then whispered in my boy's ear

Doesn't that rock looks like a top of a cave

Can you imagine a cave under it

Like a well kept secret?

My boy looked at it, and then at me

And again, and again, and suddenly

He said: Mommy, the big man would not know of it

My smile was his answer – no, He won't

Then, I outlay my idea for him
If we hide the Dummies there
And leave the place looking undisturbed
No one, but us, will ever know

My boy will always know where his Dummies are
They will rest in peace
And no one will take them away
Including my boy

Suddenly, it dawned on my boy

That he also, had to say Goodbye

I could feel his sadness, and

Hugged him tightly, offering a silent understanding

We made a ceremony
And we marked the day
We sang a song
And we let it go

I then put my boy on my shoulder
And told him – you are on top of the world
Toll and strong and grown up
Ready to step forth towards a new adventure

And like this we left the lake site

Our face looking forward

Happy to find

That it is possible to say Goodbye.

Where would you hide your dummy?

www.ingramcontent.com/pod-product-compliance
Lightning Source LLC
Chambersburg PA
CBHW041431090426

42744CB00003B/38